For my mom, who introduced me to the beauty of a Luna moth
when I was eight years old.

LAS

Celebrating all the little miracles of life!

CV

A little Luna moth egg sits on a walnut leaf.
The egg is as big as the tip of a pen.

The egg sits on the leaf for 2 weeks.

At last, a little caterpillar pops from the egg.

The caterpillar eats and eats.
The little caterpillar can eat 2 walnut leaves a day!

As the caterpillar gets bigger, its skin splits.
The caterpillar wiggles from the split skin.

The caterpillar has a bigger skin to grow into. In 4 weeks the caterpillar's body will grow to be as big as it can get.

The caterpillar spins a silk cocoon.

It rests in the cocoon for 2 to 3 weeks.

But in the cocoon the caterpillar is not resting....
The caterpillar is transforming itself.

At last, the cocoon splits and a moth wiggles from it.

As the moth exits the cocoon, its wings are little and soft. The wings must fill with liquid from the moth's body to get big.

The Luna moth rests until dusk.

At last, the Luna moth lifts up on fantastic wings to go on a hunt for a mate.

And for a week she drops little eggs onto walnut leaves…

 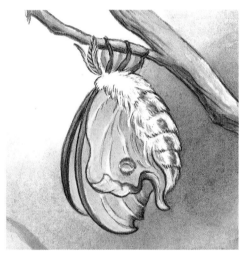 

Luna Moth is decodable with the knowledge of the 26 phonetic alphabet sounds and the ability to blend those sounds together, plus knowledge of content vocabulary pertaining to the subject matter of the story.

Puzzle Words are words used in the story that are either irregular or have sound/spelling correspondences that the reader may not be familiar with.

Please Note: If all of the puzzle words (sight words) and content words on this page are pre-taught and the reader knows the 26 phonetic alphabet sounds, and has the ability to blend those sounds together, this book is 100% phonetically decodable.

Puzzle Words	Content Words	Decodable Vocabulary:		
a	body	2	fill	resting
are	caterpillar	3	get	rests
as	cocoon	4	hunt	sits
be	eat	and	in	soft
day	eats	at	it	spins
days	grow	big	its	split
for	hunt	bigg**er**	itself	splits
from	leaf	but	last	tip
go	leaves	can	lifts	until
has	liquid	drops	litt**le**	up
into	Luna	dusk	must	wigg**les**
is	mate	egg	not	will
of	moth	eggs	on	wings
one	moth's	exits	pen	
onto	silk	fantastic	pops	
own	skin			
the	transforming			
to	walnut			
with	weeks			